MW00958003

THINGS I WANT TO

SAY AT WORK BUT CAN'T

———————————————

A FUNNY SWEAR WORD COLORING BOOK FOR ADULTS

Copyright © 2022 by Mia Waters

THIS BOOK BELONGS TO:

_____

You are truly an EPIC fucking rockstar for purchasing this book.

I really hope that you enjoy coloring in it and laugh your a$$ off too.

Oh and once you're done, I would love for you to leave a review about your experience.

Also, please be sure to check out my other selection of books.

Scan Me

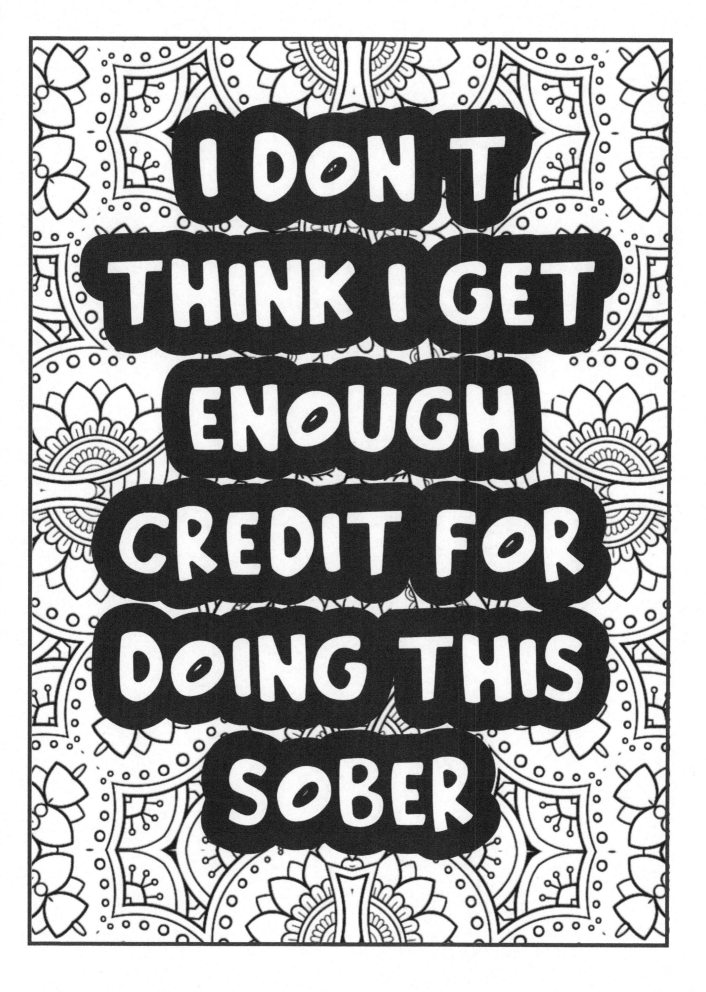

Fuck you
asshole!
how's
that for
customer
service!

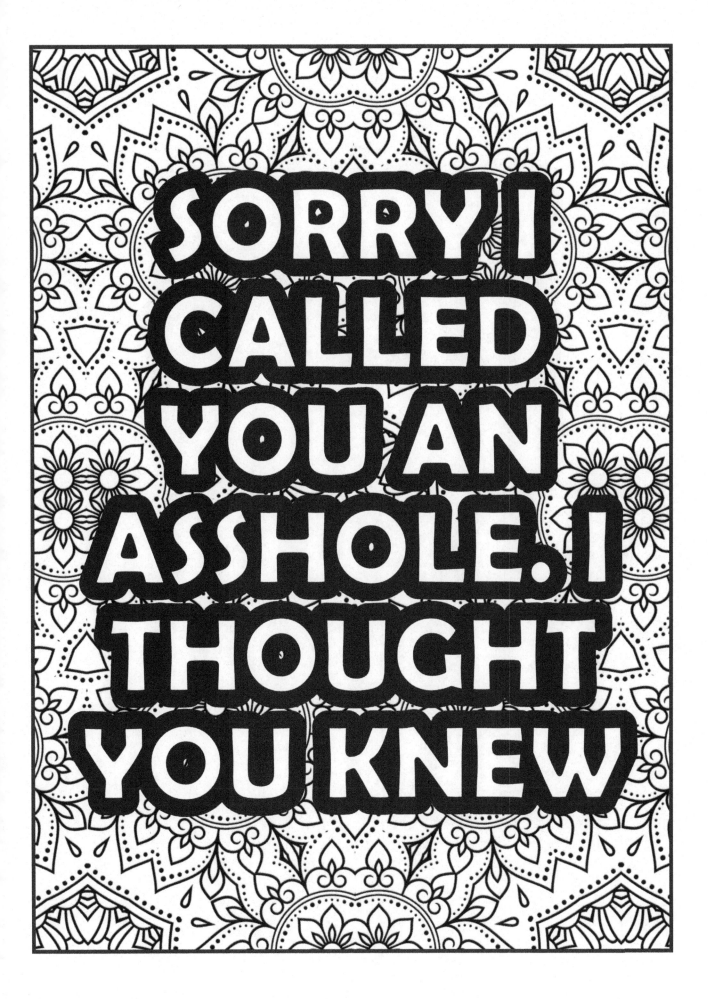

SORRY I
CALLED
YOU AN
ASSHOLE!
I THOUGHT
YOU KNEW

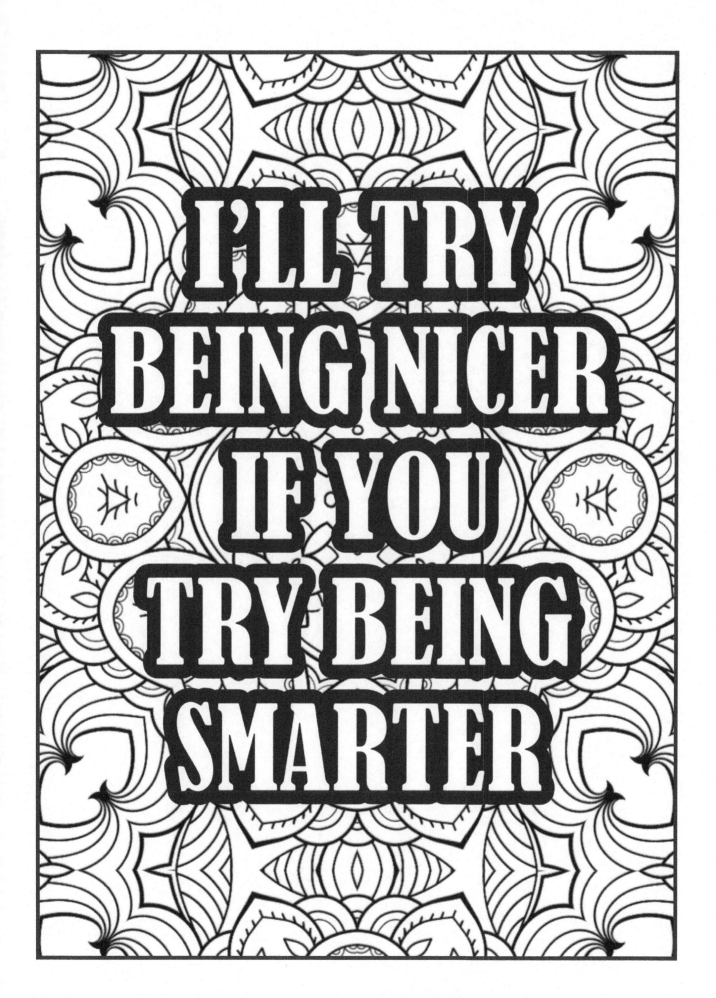

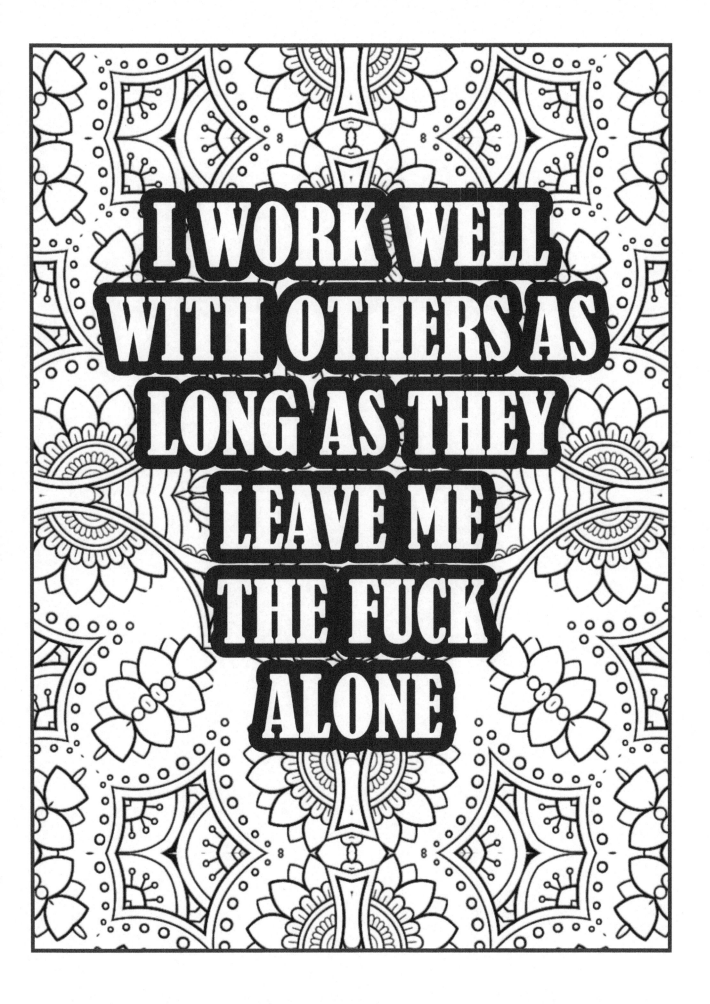

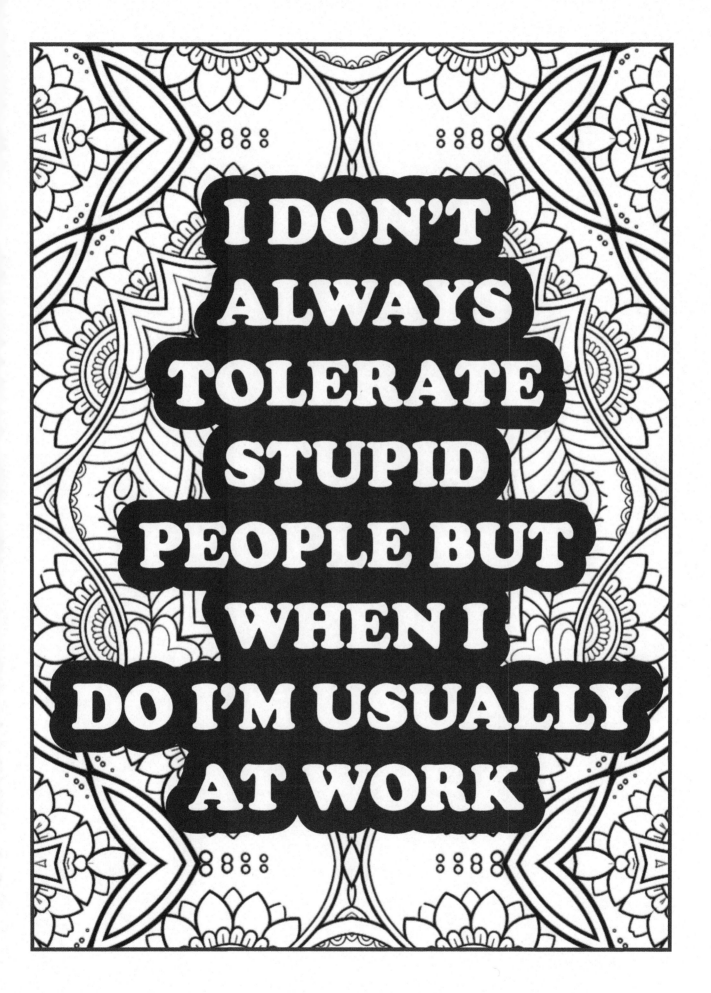

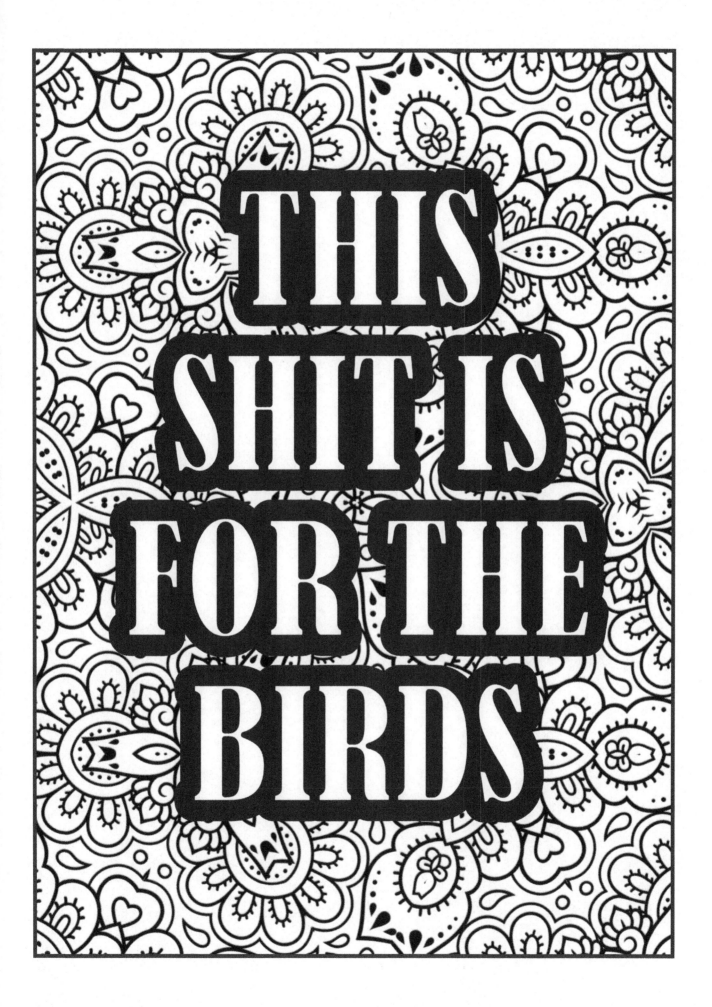

You grace

LIKE DRAMA!

get the

FUCK AWAY

from me

SHIT
SHIT
SHITTII!

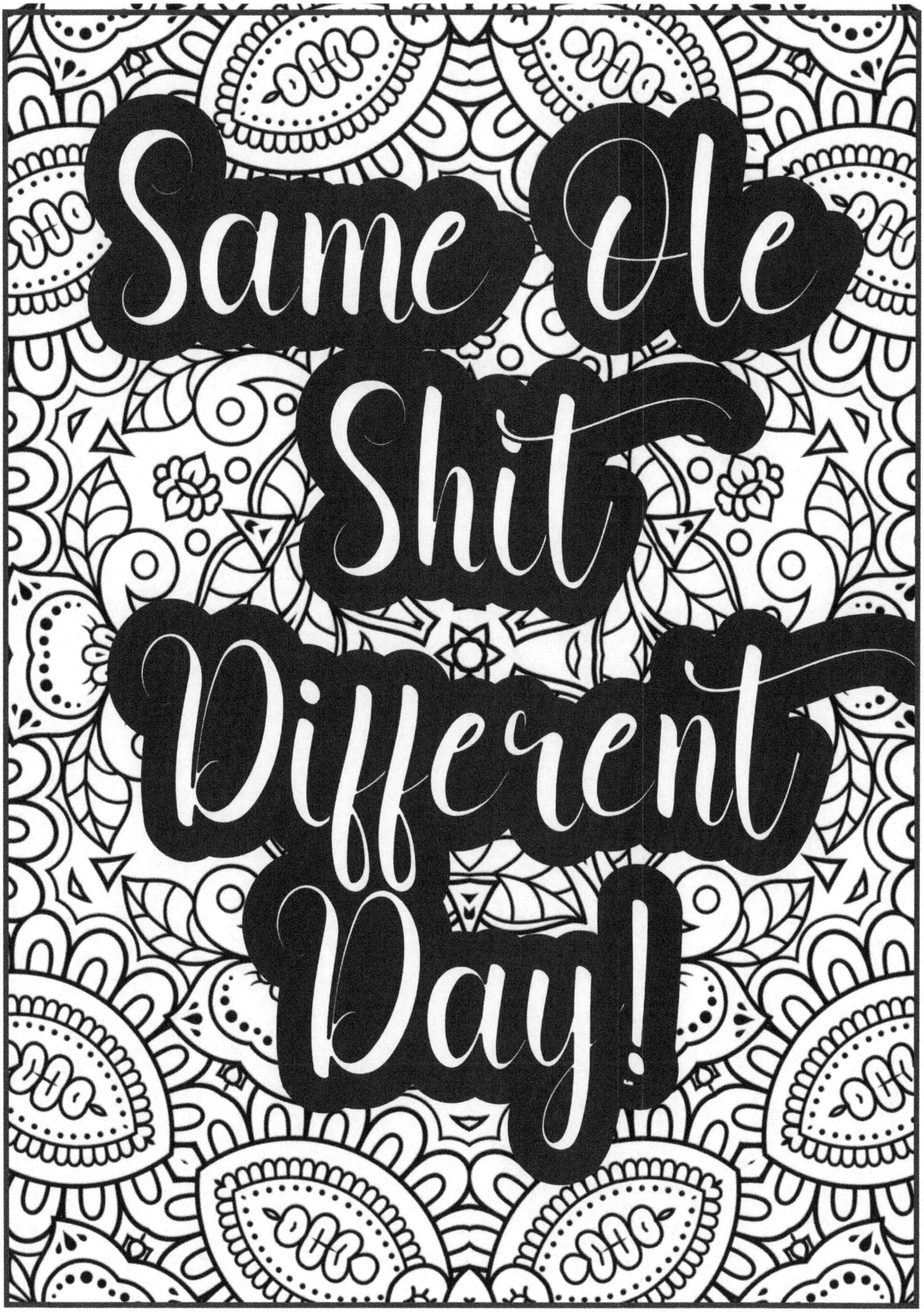
Same Ole
Shit
Different
Day!

I'M convinced WE'VE WASTED enough time ON THIS SHIT

WHO HIRED THIS BITCH?

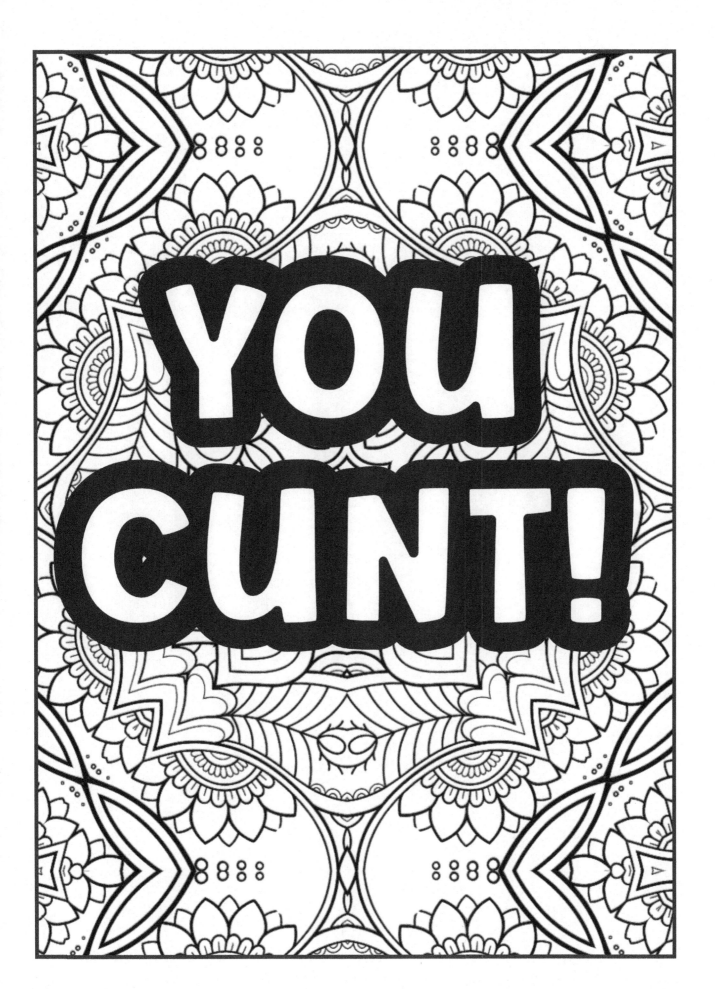

OH FOR
FUCKS
SAKE!

THANKS FOR YOUR PURCHASE!

If you enjoyed this book, I would love for you to leave a review.

Also please be sure to check out other titles in my selection of books.

Mia Waters

Made in the USA
Coppell, TX
23 December 2024

43464501R00039